This book is dedicated to my mum and dad who, in their different ways, spent their lives building God's Kingdom wherever He placed them.

Yesterday Was An Ordinary Day

Written by Jonathan Walker

"Then many will fall away, and they will betray one another, and hate one another. And many false prophets will arise and lead many astray. And because of the increase in lawlessness, the love of many will grow cold. But the one who endures to the end will be saved. And this good news of the kingdom will be proclaimed throughout the world, as a testimony to all the nations; and then the end will come."

Matthew 24: 10-14 NRSV

Introduction – The beginning of the end

It is a true saying that 'all good things must come to an end.' I had learnt that lesson every year when my family filled up our car with people, luggage, and the dog, and drove the long journey from Suffolk to Cornwall for our Summer holiday. As a child, every year in Cornwall was a 'good thing', a dream come true, a fantastic adventure. But after two weeks, the adventure always came to an end. Once or twice I managed to extend the holiday by booking a seat in the car of cousins who were leaving a few days later, but I could only delay my leaving this glorious place. I was never in a position to halt my return to the far less exciting town where I lived my normal life.

Time moves on and I grew up. In doing so, I found that Cornwall was no longer able to hold my interest. From my late teenage years I started choosing other destinations for my Summer holiday. Instead of polluting the air in an old petrol guzzling car that belched CO_2 for the long drive west, I now flew south by plane, with its ozone-busting jet engines, to a variety of Mediterranean holiday destinations. For years I was unaware and undisturbed by the knowledge that I was contributing to the death of planet earth. Probably, like many people, I was shocked when I found out for certain that this was happening. An inconvenient truth! I looked around for a solution that I could contribute to. But it gradually became apparent that the level of change needed to put things right was greater than the vast majority of people were willing to make. The politicians would announce their grand plans for fixing the problem, only to find their electors were not inclined to follow them. Many such plans were quietly dropped or modified to bring about the same change over a longer period of time. Meanwhile, the weather forecasters repeated year after year that the world was getting hotter; but people learned to ignore their message. After all, there's only so much bad news you can reasonably cope with at one time. Some put their trust in the scientists, but it soon became apparent that they did not have all the necessary solutions for returning this world to a healthier place. So people, mostly, gave up. They pushed the matter to the back of their minds and just got on with their lives as before. They, basically, did their bit to recycle, and hoped for the best. After all, we had survived many crises before...hadn't we? Perhaps we'd get through this one.

Yet still the planet continued to grow hotter, at first slowly, and then more quickly. We saw the changes in the supermarket as farmers struggled to produce sufficient food now that the weather was no longer happening as before. Through the media, we were given front row seats as we watched the planet die before our very eyes. As the situation got worse, so people became more desperate to find ways to fix the problems. Many followed leaders who promised they could easily put things right. These were the false prophets, the fake messiahs, the charlatans who saw an opportunity to manipulate people's fears in order to gain fabulous wealth for themselves. But the truth was that none of us knew if the tipping point for the environment was yet to be crossed or was already well behind us.

The Bible teaches us that when God made the whole of creation, he declared it to be 'good'[i]. Yet our planet was, even then, destined to come to an end someday. The promise of God was, come that day, something transformational would happen when Jesus returned in glory which would put all things right[ii]. So this is my story of how that world-changing event happened. I am quite sure this story will have strong similarities to others, but there will also be many variations - probably a different variation for each person. Nevertheless, I have been asked to tell you the story of how things happened to me. So let me start by introducing myself. My name is Richard Wilson, and I was thirty-six years old, a long time ago, when Jesus returned. At that time I owned a small two-bedroom terraced house in a large town called Maidstone, which is situated in the south-east corner of England. I was also the proud owner of a Tesla electric car, so I was still trying to do my bit for the environment. As a Christian, I regularly attended St Luke's Anglican church in Maidstone, and I used to have a well-paid job working as an 'Executive' for a small marketing company. Like anyone, my life was a mixture of good days and bad days, really significant days and days that quickly pass un-noticed. But then, on one unexpected day, something so huge and extraordinary happened which made all the yesterdays in my life quite ordinary by comparison.

"For as in those days before the flood they were eating and drinking, marrying and giving in marriage, until the day Noah entered the ark, and they knew nothing until the flood came and swept them all away, so too will be the coming of the Son of Man."

Matthew 24: 38 -39 NRSV

Chapter One – The weekend before

It was late on Sunday evening and what I had intended to be a very jolly occasion was struggling to be so. The high points of the evening were the moment when each of the guests arrived, especially when the birthday boy turned up. The party was meant to be a fitting celebration of my friend David's birthday, although the actual day of his birthday was on the Friday, two days before. David had dropped by early on the Friday evening because I needed him to return some tools I had lent him. I was due to be at a church meeting in an hour (to discuss important issues like the church roof, which is apparently leaking in several places), so there was enough time for a coffee and a quick catchup before going out. I brewed us both some coffee, then grabbed the packet of oat biscuits and we made ourselves comfortable in the front room. I find David is a really easy person to while away time in conversation with. On those days when I'm in the mood to share thoughts, he's a good listener, as well as someone who happens to hold interesting opinions on almost any subject. But, if I am not really in the mood to converse, I know just the right questions to ask which will keep him talking for ages, while I just sit back and relax. So the conversation on that Friday evening was going well, until I looked at my watch. David saw me do that and went quiet for a moment. I was beginning to get the impression David had something on his mind, and then it came out.

"It's actually my birthday today."

"Oh" I said, taken by surprise. "Is it a significant number?"

"It's only my thirtieth," he said, trying to make it sound like it was of no importance to him.

"Your thirtieth." I said, "Why didn't you say so before? Have you no plans to celebrate it?"

David admitted he hadn't. He explained that he never really celebrated his birthday which, come to think of it, was probably true. In the six or seven years that I had known him, I do not remember any fun event happening purely for the reason that it was David's birthday. But now that it was his birthday, and his thirtieth, it seemed to me that it ought to be celebrated. But there wasn't time that evening because I had this meeting to go to, which I really couldn't get out of. Then tomorrow I was leaving early to drive to a friend's wedding on the far side of London and then staying over at the reception venue. So I'd be back late Sunday afternoon, which meant that Sunday evening was the first possible time I could organise some sort of suitable social gathering.

"David, why don't you come round here on Sunday evening," I said to him. "Shall we say Seven thirty?...and I'll cook us a meal to celebrate your birthday." As I said these words I was already thinking of people I could invite. But since I didn't know if anyone would be available to join us for the evening, I decided not to mention the idea of others joining us. But hopefully there would be a few people available to come.

Saturday was a long day. I left home early so that I could be at the church by 10 am. The wedding was due to start at 11 am, but the groom wanted his ushers to be there nice and early so we could spend a little time together in a local coffee shop. At least, that was what he said. It may have just been his way of ensuring we were all at the wedding on time.

Weddings were pretty familiar to me. By the age of thirty-six, I had lost all count of the number of weddings I had attended, and they can blur a bit in my memory. But, having said that, this was a very happy wedding, and quite a splash-out. At a time when weddings were generally becoming smaller events due to the astronomical rise in the cost of food and drink, this wedding was not the norm. The bride's parents were said to be loaded, and with only one child's wedding to pay for. I didn't really know the bride's family, but they seemed nice, and generous people. The groom was a friend from university, and he had been through some difficult times when it came to life in general, and more specifically in finding himself a wife. This was partly due to him being in a car accident which had left him paralysed. But after ten years of hard work with physiotherapists and regular access to a sophisticated exoskeleton, you would hardly have known he had any disability. Watching him dance with his bride in the ballroom of the rather grand hotel really put a smile on everyone's faces, as well as a few tears in their eyes.

During the wedding reception, when my attention wasn't needed elsewhere, I took the opportunity to message friends back home in Maidstone. I was feeling quite pleased with myself having found seven people who were available to come to my house on the Sunday. I told them to arrive well before David so that, as I opened the front door to let him in they could all shout 'SURPRISE!' Okay, so that wasn't exactly an original idea, but I thought David would appreciate it. As it happened, my plan went well, and David seemed very happy to see everyone. So, at this point everything was going just fine. But then I made the mistake of choosing to turn on the radio to provide relaxing background music. It was just laziness on my part. Normally I would have gone through my on-line music collection and made a specific selection for the occasion; the right songs to create the right mood. But on this occasion I just turned on the radio and chose a station that specialises in easy listening music. That was fine, I liked the music they played. But then 8 pm came around and with it the ten minutes of home and international news.

I had just finished serving up the stir-fry and noodles that I'd been cooking when the news came on. If there was anything likely to spoil the mood of any party these days, it was the news. There seldom seemed to be any good news, and that Sunday evening was no exception. On the home news front, the main story was the declining health of the king. He had been battling cancer for some time and it now looked like he was losing the war. That story was what initially grabbed people's attention. I would have immediately turned off he news, except that everyone had stopped talking and were listening to the radio. Then came the International news and there were riots in Israel over the work of rebuilding the Temple in Jerusalem.

This was an interesting story. It turned out that some years ago the Ark of the Covenant had been discovered in a cave close to where it was thought the original Temple had been. The Israeli government immediately took control over the site and made the archaeologist who found it swear to tell no one about his find. Then the government put together a team of experts, who were also sworn to secrecy, and whose first job was to decide if this really was the original Ark. I have no expertise on this subject, but apparently, after a variety of checks were made, the experts came to the unanimous conclusion that it was the genuine article. Having been lost for over two thousand five hundred years, the Ark of the Covenant was finally back in the hands of the Jewish people. Having received this conclusion from the group of experts, the Israeli government decided that they still had to keep this find a secret whilst they thought about what to do with it. To have this debate, more people had to be sworn to secrecy. Leaders from all wings of the Jewish religious community had to be consulted without any word getting out to the general public. Amazingly, the government successfully completed its consultation without there being any news leak, and the conclusion was fairly universal. Although everyone agreed that this was the Ark of the Covenant, there was some disagreement as to what should be done with it. Some thought it should go into a museum. Others thought it was too precious to be placed in a museum. In their view, the original Ark should be stored away somewhere totally safe, with an exact copy on display in a museum. But the majority of experts and religious leaders thought that the only right thing to do with the Ark was re-house it at the centre of a new great Temple in Jerusalem; the plans for which already existed.

This was when the Israeli government discovered that what they had done thus far was the easy bit. Where things got really difficult was in finding a suitable site on which to build the Temple. This was the point where word got out that the Ark had been found and the plan was to place it in a re-built Temple. There weren't many possible sites in Jerusalem which were large enough for this project, and each site had its opposers, whether Jewish, Muslim or Christian. Eventually, the site was chosen, and work got started. The construction of the Temple was done, as much as was possible, according to instructions in the Bible. But nothing could be done to satisfy the Muslim community which claimed the land had special significance to their religion and vigorously campaigned against its building. But at this point in our story, the Temple project is now at a very advanced stage and there seem to be increasingly violent riots every day in the streets of Jerusalem because of it.

The next story on the news was the continuing investigation over the two huge ships that had recently been attacked and sunk in the Mediterranean, losing their cargo of wheat. With wheat now selling on the open market at unheard of prices, organised crime had seen an opportunity to make a lot of money. Rather than working together, each criminal organisation made their deals with cargo ship companies to protect their ships whilst doing what they could to sink their opponents ships. By doing this they kept the price of wheat sky high. Millions of people in the poorer arts of the world were dying of starvation, but that wasn't bothering those who ran these criminal businesses. Food security had become a massive issue around the world now that crops had failed to some degree or other in every country. Only the richest countries were able to buy sufficient food for their own people, but this meant that they didn't have the spare money to spend on navies that could defend the cargo ships. So the high seas had become a place for gangsters and pirates. Cruise ships had become a thing of the past as they were an easy target for those who wanted to take hostages for ransom.

Meanwhile, the world was continuing to get hotter…as people's hearts grew colder. The heat caused wild fires and the destruction of nature, the mass extinction of animal life and the relocation of people away from those areas of the world that had become virtually uninhabitable. Meanwhile, fear of those who were homeless, hungry and worst of all, foreign, grew in the hearts of those who had just enough to get by. Fear that the little they had would be taken from them and given to those who had nothing. There was a new story about these troubled times every single day. Could humans save the planet or was it too late? Had we already passed the tipping point? There was no way of knowing.

I breathed a sigh of relief when the news section came to an end and the music began again. But I couldn't shake off the sense of guilt I had about being a citizen of one of the wealthiest countries. A country that could, for perhaps longer than others, avoid some of the worst suffering that a large part of the world was having to cope with. As the conversation turned to these subjects it was easy to forget that we had gathered together that evening for a celebration. So I raised a glass to drink a toast to David and his thirty years of life. The others rallied in their moods and raised their glasses with me. May David have thirty more years of happy life, we declared, though none of us really thought that was likely given the circumstances .

The end of the party came quite quickly. After all, it was Sunday night. People had work to go to in the morning. So, as soon as the first person said they were going all the others began to look at their watches and acknowledged that they too needed to leave. Only my friend Mike stopped behind. He clearly wanted to talk, and it was a warm evening, so we went out into the back garden. My garden was narrow, but quite long, and I had recently placed a bench at the far end which was a little more private than the rest of the garden. We sat down and were silent for a while, finishing off our drinks and looking up at the few stars that are visible when you live in a large town. Then our discussion began with me asking Mike the same question I had asked him many times before, "So, Mike, what's happening with you and Paula these days? I did ask her along to this evening's party. I thought you'd want me to. But she couldn't make it."

Mike didn't exactly sigh, but he did make a noise that demonstrated his exasperation.

"I can't make her out," he said, "It is literally...one moment she's full-on friendly...flashing her eyes at me, and the next moment she just doesn't want to know. I don't know what to make of her."

"Perhaps you just need to play things a little more cool," I said, trying to be helpful.

"I've done that, and then she's all over me like a rash, asking me why I'm ignoring her."

"And what do you say to her when she asks you that?"

"I don't know what to say. I just end up denying that I'm ignoring her and leaving it there."

"Look, you're both adults, why don't you two just sit down together and tell the truth about your feelings for each other? This 'will they, won't they' thing has been going on for ages."

"It's just not so easy as that. The problem is that I don't really know how much I like her. Of course, there are some things that I really like about her...but I don't like the fact that she seems so undecided about me."

"Perhaps she's undecided about you because she senses you're undecided about her."

"Hmmm. Maybe."

"So, that's why the two of you might benefit from an open and frank conversation about what you think of each other." I then laughed and said, "I'd be happy to act as a referee."

Mike also laughed. "No thank you," he said. "What kind of turnip-head would I look like if I needed someone to referee Paula and my conversation?"

"Good point."

There was silence for a moment. Neither of us knowing what to say next. But, eventually, Mike spoke, "Why can't it just be straight forward...I like her, and she likes me...and we can just get on with having a relationship. My parents were like that. They met on the first day of Secondary school, and they were an item from then on."

"Yes, that sounds very idyllic and easy," I said wistfully. "But, I think, for that to work, they must have been the sort of people who were ready to settle down just as soon as they reached adulthood. I could never have done that."

"Maybe...but if someone is the right person for you, and you want to, for example, explore the world before settling down...then they'd probably go and explore the world with you. That's part of what would make them right for you, isn't it?"

"You're probably right," I said, "I guess I'm just jealous of people who seem to find someone so quickly and easily. Here I am, at the age of thirty-six, still looking for someone. Every time I go to a social gathering, or even to church on a Sunday, I find myself looking around in case there is somebody new to check out. I can't help it. I do it automatically. It bothers me that I do that. I really want to 'check out' from checking people out!" We both laughed. "So, has your parent's marriage been a happy one?" I asked.

"As far as I can tell. That's always been my impression. But you never really know for sure. By the way, have I told you that my dad is dying of cancer."

"No, you haven't. I'm sorry to hear that. Didn't I meet your dad some years ago?"

"Yes, my mum and dad both came to my Baptism. I introduced you."

"Yes, I remember now. Isn't he a minister or vicar or something?"

"At that time he was dean of Ely Cathedral, but he's retired now."

"So...when you say he is dying of cancer..."

"It's prostate cancer. You have to catch it early, but in his case they didn't catch it early enough."

"How long are the doctors saying he's got?"

"They reckon he's got no more than a few months. He's one of those people who won't see a doctor unless they are feeling like they're at death's door...which is a bad approach when it comes to cancer."

"Well, I am very sorry about that. And it will be very hard on your mum when your dad dies, having had very little experience of living alone before now." At this point I could think of nothing else to say. So there was another pause in the conversation before Mike spoke again.

"Have you got both your parents?"

"No, just my mum," I said, "My dad died of a heart attack almost ten years ago. It was very quick. I barely had time to say goodbye."

"So did you manage to say goodbye?"

"Yes...I did...just."

I guess our conversation could have gone on for much longer than this, but it was late on a Sunday evening, and I had had a very busy weekend. I was also expecting an equally challenging week ahead of me at work. So, we chatted just a little longer as we walked back up the garden and through the house. I waved as mike drove away and walked back inside. It was then that I noticed I had a whole stack of washing up to do. My kitchen was not big enough for a dish washer. Well, that could wait till the morning. Right now, all I wanted to do was go to bed and sleep. So I did.

"Star of wonder, *star* of night.

Star with royal beauty bright.

Westward leading, still proceeding.

Guide us to thy Perfect *Light*."

We three Kings by John Henry Hopkins Jr

Chapter Two – Monday morning

When the clock radio beside my bed reached 7 am, a gentle waking up process began. No loud and over excited radio DJs to start my day. Just snatches of the news headlines, at first on low volume, but gradually getting louder, reminding me that the world of wakefulness was not going to allow me to sleep forever. I was still too blurry to be focussed on what was being said. Besides, I heard the news late last night before I went to bed. Could anything major have happened since then?

The first news headline was that there had been no update about the condition of the king. I consider myself slightly more Royalist than Republican, but I felt I could do without endless conversation about why there was nothing new to say about the king's health. Still, I lay in bed a little bit longer to see what the next story would be. My brain was still in two minds about waking up when I heard just a snippet of a headline that I did not recognise, "Scientists have been trying to work out what this strange phenomena in the sky actually is." The volume on my radio went down again, as if it were teasing me...because I was interested now. A few more seconds and, at last, the radio was now up to its regular volume. Meanwhile, the news presenter had finished reading the headlines and had settled into a story about the huge number of immigrants making their way across Europe wishing to settle in the UK. I must admit, I have never experienced anything like the hunger or destitution that these people had...so how could blame them? I couldn't. But that wasn't the story I wanted to hear about. What was this "strange phenomena in the sky" that I heard in the headlines? That sounded like an interesting story. As I climbed out of bed and went to the bathroom, I kept listening to the radio in case they began talking about it.

Eventually, the story came round. But, it turned out, there wasn't much to say, and what they did say just left me confused. It reminded me of a conversation I once had with my Managing Director about the day the Twin Towers were brought down by two planes. On that day, my boss was working in an office in London when the news came over the radio that one of the Twin Towers in New York had been hit by a plane. With no more information than that, those who shared the office with him were confused about what had really happened. A plane had crashed into one of the Twin Towers? What sort of plane are we talking about here? For a short while they thought the story was of a small, two seater aeroplane which had accidentally slammed into the sky scraper. It took a few minutes before they realised that the radio presenter meant a Jumbo Jet full of people. In that moment the story changed into something far bigger and more horrible...and completely unlike what they had originally thought. So I listened to the radio, and heard the BBC presenter, Nathan Trimble, interviewing their Science correspondent Rebekah Swithers, and this is what I heard...

Nathan Trimble: Scientists around the world are looking at a strange phenomenon in the sky that was first seen just after 2 am this morning. There is some speculation that this is a particularly slow moving comet, but no one has ever seen a comet move as slowly as this one. Here is our science correspondent, Rebekah Swithers, to explain what it is people are seeing. So, Rebekah, what have we got here?

Rebekah Swithers: Well, I wish I could explain, Nathan. But at this moment in time no one knows what it is we're looking at.

NT: There has been talk of space junk creating this effect...is that likely?

RS:Not according to the scientists I have talked to. But, on the other hand, no one is ruling anything out.

NT: What about the possibility that we are looking at a UFO? A space ship from another planet?

RS:Well, given the fact that we have, so far, been unable to identify what this is...we can say with some level of certainty that it is an Unidentified Flying Object. But whether or not it is a space ship from another planet...no one knows. What scientists have found is that this source of light seems to have no mass to it. So, a rock, or a piece of space debris that was either reflecting the sun's light, or creating light by burning up in the atmosphere, would have to be a solid thing. Obviously, if it was burning up, then that solid thing would be getting smaller as it burns. But this light we are seeing amongst the Northern Lights has no discernible mass...which is leaving scientists baffled. All our scientific tools like lasers and radar tell us there is nothing there, yet we can see it with our eyes.

NT: So, Rebekah, will we be able to see this light for ourselves?

RS:Yes, we think the light is moving. As I said earlier, the star or light was first seen amongst the Northern Lights in Norway, Finland, and northern parts of Russia and Canada, but it looks like it is slowly moving south. So everyone should be able to see it from anywhere in the UK sometime between 10:30 and 11:15 this morning.

NT: You'll be able to see it in the daylight then?

RS:Oh yes. It's a very bright light. It should be visible through the clouds as well.

NT: Could it damage our eyes if we looked directly at it?

RS:Er, no, the scientists I have spoken to don't think it will. It's not like the sun in that respect. But having said that, since we don't actually know what it is we are looking at, we don't really know what will happen if you stare at it for any length of time. So, probably best not do that.

NT: Ok. Thanks Rebekah. The time is seventeen minutes past seven. We'll find out what the weather forecast is in just under ten minutes time, but in the meantime... Controversy in the Houses of Parliament yesterday afternoon when a member of parliament, and chairman of the Foreign Affairs committee...

I turned off the radio and hurried downstairs to power up my tablet so I could now watch the TV news as I ate my breakfast in the kitchen. I'm really into things to do with outer space, which was why the story had grabbed my attention. I was hoping for a reasonable, scientific explanation for the light. But sadly, no theory had yet emerged. At least I was able to see on the tablet what they were talking about. It really did look like a star. I even checked out some of the other news channels. They were all talking about the star but none of them had anything new to say. Then I looked at my watch and realised I had run out of time. No time to make sandwiches for my lunch. Just time to grab my coat, phone and wallet before dashing out of my house and driving off to work.

It was my habit to listen to podcasts as I drove to work in the morning, but today I couldn't concentrate on what the speaker was saying. The phrase, 'Star in the sky', stuck in my head because it reminded me of the star over Bethlehem when Jesus was born. People have speculated about what exactly the Christmas star was. There were various possibilities including a comet, or a supernova (an exploding star). Whatever this mysterious 'star' was, the thought that it might be the same as the star that sat over Bethlehem two thousand years ago was really exciting. As a Christian, I believed that Jesus would one day return. But surely it couldn't be happening now? Was this 'star' really God's way of announcing that the day had arrived? I wanted the answer to be 'yes', but I was struggling to believe it. I felt an adrenalin rush several times on the half-hour journey to work as the thought that we really might be about to experience the end of this corrupt world, sank in.

The company I work for is a small marketing business named after its founder and Managing Director Anthony Herrington - 'Herrington Marketing'. It takes up half a floor in a newly built, three storey office block. Most of us have a room of our own, but two of the guys share. The MD has the largest office which doubles up as a conference room. Most of my work colleagues, like me, are in their thirties, with only the MD in his mid-fifties. Although we cover all areas of marketing, our speciality is the organising of events. So, if a business or charity want to raise their profile through an event, that's when they might call on us for help. I have done this sort of work since leaving university and I enjoy it, but I lack the ambition that drives most of my work colleagues.

I arrived at the office ten minutes early and messaged a few friends and family whilst I powered up my PC and made myself a coffee. I wanted to find out what they thought of the star. Then I checked the on-line news. They now had some up-close film of the star taken by a United States military plane designed to fly on the edge of the atmosphere. But apart from confirming that the light was there, there was still no obvious explanation for it.

By now, responses to my messaging were coming in. Most of them were brief comments, agreeing with me that this was all pretty weird, but no one expressed any opinions about what the star in the sky might signify. Except for one, a cousin of mine, "It reminds me of the star over Bethlehem," he wrote. "Yes!" I said out loud. "At least I'm not the only one who thinks that." I had just under half an hour before the star was expected to be visible from where we were, so it was time to try to focus my mind on work, which proved to be really difficult. I must have looked at the clock on the wall at least twenty times in that half an hour. When the time came, I happily dropped what I was doing and joined a growing crowd of people outside. The whole company was gathering there, including the MD, which was a bit of a surprise. There were also people from all the other businesses that used the same building. People were mostly standing in groups of twos, threes and fours chatting away excitedly, until the star drifted over the northern horizon.

For perhaps a minute or two all conversation stopped. There was something incredibly beautiful about the star. It was bright, but not so that it hurt our eyes, and it was a very white star. It moved across the sky in the way that a satellite can sometimes be seen at night. In fact, the first words which broke the silence came from one of our staff who said, "It must be some new form of satellite that no government is admitting to having put up there." His was the first of many suggestions. In fact there was quite a range of response to this amazing sight. Whilst some people appeared to have a casual interest in what was going on, others seemed to be taking it very seriously. A few people looked troubled or anxious whilst some of the younger lads in our company made a joke of it with talk of monster aliens that were preparing to invade the earth. I put this down to the many hours they spent playing computer games. But no one was really laughing. Most people were taking this strange star in the sky seriously. Nobody mentioned the Bethlehem star. I hadn't really expected that they would, yet it was this possibility which was 'front and centre' of my mind.

I returned to my computer and checked the news again before getting on with my work. The people on the news channel were saying how surprised they were that the star could be seen through the clouds. But then one reporter, talking to the news channel presenter, made this comment, "It's as if someone or something was wanting us all to see this light," and I thought, "Yes, it is, isn't it?"

Even before the star had disappeared over the southern horizon, people outside our building had started to drift back to their offices, and conversations came to an end. I found that I was already beginning to tire of the same few ideas about the star that went round and round in the conversations on the news. I was hoping that the lunchtime news would have had the time to discover something new about the star. With all the other significant news stories going on. Could they find new information or a new angle on this story?

"Then Jesus said to him, 'Someone gave a great dinner and invited many. At the time for the dinner he sent his slave to say to those who had been invited, "Come; for everything is ready now." But they all alike began to make excuses. The first said to him, "I have bought a piece of land, and I must go out and see it; please accept my apologies." Another said, "I have bought five yoke of oxen, and I am going to try them out; please accept my apologies." Another said, "I have just been married, and therefore I cannot come." So the slave returned and reported this to his master. Then the owner of the house became angry and said to his slave, "Go out at once into the streets and lanes of the town and bring in the poor, the crippled, the blind, and the lame." And the slave said, "Sir, what you ordered has been done, and there is still room." Then the master said to the slave, "Go out into the roads and lanes, and compel people to come in, so that my house may be filled. For I tell you, none of those who were invited will taste my dinner."

Luke 14: 16 - 24

Chapter Three – Monday afternoon and evening

The radio news programme I regularly listened to as I ate my lunch had made it the third story. The king's health was the first story. An official announcement from Buckingham Palace just said that the king had slept well through the night, which didn't really tell us anything. But what was more telling was the fact that the whole royal family were, at that very moment, heading towards Windsor Castle, which is where the king had been living recently. So all those who were interviewed on the radio, claiming to be royal insiders, were speculating that the king did not have much time left.

The second story was on climate change, and a new report that had come out of the United Nations calling on everybody and every government to do anything and everything they could to halt the decline in the weather around the world. "Time is running out!" said the UN General Secretary. 'So,' I thought to myself, 'time is running out for the king AND the planet.' The symmetry was interesting, and the scientists interviewed for this part of the programme were also sounding pretty despondent. "We have a whole bunch of tipping points," one of them said, "and we simply don't know which ones we have already crossed."

So the strange star in the sky had become the third story, and the radio news programme had clearly decided to tackle the story from all angles. The first guest interviewed was a top UK astronomer. He was bluntly asked to explain exactly what was happening out there on the fringes of our atmosphere, and tell us if we should be worried about it? He was unable to answer either of these questions. Then an army general was asked for his perspective on this situation. Could this be a solid sign that there really were aliens eyeing up our planet, and are we capable of defending ourselves from them if we were attacked? He seemed to think we should be okay...but I couldn't help feeling he was bluffing.

The next person to be interviewed was a Church of England Bishop. She was asked if she thought this was some sort of sign from God. I had the impression that the interviewer wasn't very interested in what the Bishop had to say and seemed genuinely surprised when she said, "Yes, I think it is a sign of some sort." However, the Bishop also seemed very reluctant to say what she thought the 'sign' was meant to be telling us. I concluded that the people making the programme were not very comfortable with having 'God' on their show, but they knew a lot of their listeners still believed in God, so they had to cover that angle. What caught ME by surprise was that after the Bishop had said her piece, the Imam of a London mosque was asked what he thought was going on. "You know," he said, "many Muslims believe in the second coming of Jesus, and until we know otherwise, I think the star in the sky might be a sign that this is about to happen." For a moment the news presenter didn't know how to respond.

"So...you...believe in Jesus?"

"We believe that he is a great prophet who will return to the earth on Judgement day," replied the rather confident-sounding Imam.

It occurred to me that the radio presenter was deeply uncomfortable with the words 'judgement day' because she began a follow-up question, but gave up on it, claiming they had run out of time. She then turned to Simon Worthing, the man who was waiting to tell us about the weather, and said, "So, Simon, what's your judgement on the weather today?"

After my lunch break, with the afternoon stretched out before me, I knew that I had to somehow focus on my work. With a little effort, I managed to do that. But then, around 4 pm I received an email from the priest at my church. He was asking everyone to come to church that evening to talk and pray about this light in the sky. I wasn't surprised to have received this email. I knew that my priest would have some thoughts of his own to share, and I could understand him not wanting to do so in an email. This needed to be talked about within the church family, so I was happy to go.

Later, when I returned home from work and put on the TV, I checked the Guide to see what was on that evening. I noticed that several channels had changed their programme schedule to include films like "Independence Day" and "Armageddon". Films that showed threats to the world from outer space. But I wasn't convinced about the idea of invading aliens. It didn't make any sense to me. I believed that this is God's world, for which he has a purpose, and I couldn't see how aliens had any part to play in it.

I quickly made myself some supper and then went to the evening meeting at church. I anticipated that a certain group in the church which some of us jokingly referred to as, 'The Prophets' would be particularly fired up by this star. There was a lot of 'longing' for the second coming in this group. But what I was wanting were the kind of sensible, well thought out comments I was expecting to get from my priest. His was the opinion I really respected. Whilst I knew 'The Prophets' would feel certain that some significant event was about to happen, I was still open to there being a straight forward scientific explanation for the light. In fact, I was really torn over which option I preferred. Let me show you what I mean.

As I was sipping a coffee from the refreshment bar at the back of the church, I got into a conversation with Tom who led the worship at church. It was only a brief conversation because he was getting ready to start the meeting with some worship songs. I thought that he'd be pretty certain about this star being a sign from God, but it turned out he didn't really think like that. He had an older brother who was a Professor in Astrophysics at Sheffield University, and he was one of a small group of scientists that the UK government had quickly put together to investigate this new phenomenon. Apparently, James (his brother) was very excited about this new object, but purely from a scientific perspective. He had assured Tom that it would be only a matter of days before they worked out what it was. Tom told me that James was not a believer in Jesus, but he was clearly very bright, and Tom seemed to take his opinion seriously. So I must admit that, by the end of my conversation with Tom I was feeling quite discouraged. If the star was just going to be a trick of the light, or something no more significant than that, then I would have been getting excited for nothing. Like getting excited about Christmas only to find that, at the last minute, the whole family had gone down with a tummy bug and Christmas was cancelled.

On the other hand, if my conversation with Tom had been different. If he hadn't had a Professor in Astrophysics for a brother. If he had been quite certain that this star was a sign from God, that would have been really great...except...what about my friend who had just got married and was looking forward to many years of happiness with his wife? Thinking about it, nearly everybody I knew had hopes and dreams for the future which would not now be fulfilled, at least in this life. And I was no exception. Having these kind of thoughts meant that I wasn't sure which I wanted more. Yes, there was a big part of me that would welcome the second coming. But there was also a significant part of me that was hoping it wasn't going to happen just yet.

In fact, something else happened which just added to the muddle going on inside my brain. I had just sat down in the main body of the church, ready for the meeting to start, when along came Paula. She had only just arrived at church, and she asked if the seat beside me was taken. It wasn't, so she sat there. This was the same Paula whom Mike had been talking about after the Sunday evening party. We chatted briefly.

Paula had only moved to Maidstone six months previous, which is when both I and Mike met her for the first time. However, the difference between us was that Mike fell instantly in love with her, whereas I just thought she was nice. Human relationships are much more complicated when there are strong feelings involved. Perhaps I have some sort of aversion to complicated relationships, but I had spent many years watching other people's relationships form and either go on to marriage or fall apart with much heart break and tears. At this stage there was no way of me knowing which way Mike and Paula's relationship was going to go. But, obviously, I wished the best for the both of them.

Then the meeting began, and it turned out to be very calm and peaceful. The priest talked about people's fears and drew from 1 John 4: 18,"There is no fear in love. But perfect love drives out fear because fear has to do with punishment. The one who fears is not made perfect in love." He went on to say that God does not want us to be afraid, but to trust in his love. We then got into small groups to pray for the world. Then, unexpectedly, Mike arrived at the end of the meeting, having previously told me he couldn't make it. He sat down on the other side of Paula. They both seemed happy to see each other, so when the meeting had finished I left Paula to tell Mike about what had been said before he arrived, and I went home.

As I drove through Maidstone at the end of the meeting, it occurred to me that I could all too easily be fearful about being single. Was the fact that I seldom did anything to win a fair maiden going to leave me a life-long bachelor? Getting married was still on my checklist of things I wanted to do. Should I be concerned about not achieving this, or any other of my dreams or ambitions because the world as we know it was about to end? Or does a relationship with Jesus mean that we, inevitably, have to let go of everything else...and believe that God can and will ensure that any loss in this life will be far outweighed by the gains of the next? There was almost too much to think about.

When I arrived home and was putting out my wheelie bin for the Council lorry to empty the next morning, I was joined by my next door neighbour, who was doing the same thing. Brian was a Jehovah's Witness and a very friendly guy. He had long since given up trying to convert me, and I wasn't trying to convert him. So with that understanding, we had arrived at a place where we could chat freely about our similarities and differences. We would often have interesting conversations over the garden fence about what was happening in the news, to which our respective faiths gave us different perspectives. But generally, we found, there was much more that we agreed on than disagreed on. Obviously, we discussed the star, and I had the impression that he was pretty happy about it being a sign from God, but I was feeling unsettled. It was a warm night, so we were both happy standing outside and chatting for a while about the differences in the way our two churches were approaching the 'star' issue. But then tiredness began to take over. It had been a mentally stressful day, so I needed to go to bed. Brian, I think, could see that I was tired and so he finished what he was saying. Then we shook hands, bid each other 'good night', and went back into our own houses.

When I went to bed, I spent a little while just placing myself and other friends and family into God's hands for safe keeping. I specifically prayed for Mike and Paula, that God would determine what happened there...and for my neighbour, Brian, and his family. Whilst I was due to see Mike the next day, in the evening, we weren't able to discuss how that encounter with Paula had gone. This was a shame because they did seem to be getting on very well. After that, as you will see, the return of Jesus Christ into the world probably determined what happened between them. As it happens, I have yet to meet either of them, or my JW neighbour since that time. However, I am optimistic that I will see them again someday. Then I went to sleep.

"Those who are ashamed of me and of my words in this adulterous and sinful generation, of them the Son of Man will also be ashamed when he comes in the glory of his Father with the holy angels."

Mark 8: 38 NRSV

Chapter Four – Tuesday morning

I woke the next morning just after 6:30 am. So I still had half an hour before my clock radio switched on at 7 am. I tried to go back to sleep. But as soon as I remembered the star I knew my chances of falling asleep again were pretty slim. Sure enough, after a few more minutes of lying in bed, I got up, put on my dressing gown and slippers, and went downstairs to make myself a cup of tea. As I was waiting for the kettle to boil the phone rang. I looked at the kitchen clock. It was 6:43 am. Who on earth would be phoning me at this time of the morning?

"Hello?" I said, keeping it brief.

"Richard. It's your cousin Paul here."

"Paul...to what do I owe this pleasure?"

"I'm doing the Lord's work today...and I was wondering if I could drop in for a spot of breakfast?" Now, my cousin, Paul, lives in the county of Suffolk and I live in Kent.

"That would be great, Paul, but I have to go to work today. By the time you get here I'll be gone."

"Oh, I don't think so," he said.

"Why, where are you?"

"Parked outside your house."

I went into the front sitting room and drew back the curtain. Sure enough, there was Paul grinning at me in his car which was parked beside mine on the drive in front of my house. He had his phone in one hand and was waving at me with his other, and there was another man in the car sitting next to Paul.

"Who's your friend?" I asked.

"This is my very new-found friend, and fellow traveller. His name is Willard (Willard waved), and he's from America. May we come in?"

"Yes, of course."

The two men climbed out of the car as I unlocked and opened the front door.

"Hello. Hello." said Paul leading the way. "This is Willard" he reminded me…knowing how bad I was at names

"Yes. Hello Willard. How do you guys know each other?"
"Well, we don't really," Paul answered. "In fact, we only met earlier this morning at the Thurrock motorway service station."

"Oh."

"Willard flew into England last night and managed to get a lift to the service station, which was where I met him."

"Where are you going to Willard?"

"I'm trying to get to Jerusalem, but there were no seats available directly to Israel…or anywhere near Israel, so at the last minute I jumped on a flight to England. At least it got me over the Atlantic.

Then, as Paul said, I managed to hitch a ride with someone to the service station, which was where I met Paul."

"Coffee break...I had an urgent need for coffee" Paul said looking in the direction of my kitchen. "Anyway, it turned out that we were both on a journey to the same place."

"Jerusalem?" I asked.

"Yes," they both replied.

"So, Paul kindly offered me a lift in his car."

"And Willard kindly offered to help with the cost of keeping it charged up," Paul said, "which reminds me, cousin, can I plug in while we're here?"

"Sure, help yourself. I think my charger will have you filled up in no time," I said. Then I headed towards the kitchen. "Do you guys want eggs and bacon, or cereal, or toast, or what?"

Back in the kitchen, I powered up the tablet so that we could have the news on in the background. The first story I heard them talk about was of an elderly couple who were killed by a tree falling on them in a storm they had over Bristol the previous evening.

"We have a lot of storms in America these days," Willard said, "and each seems worse than the previous ones." He had come into the kitchen to see if he could help with preparing the breakfast.

"Yes, our weather is getting worse each year" I said. "If you could keep an eye on the eggs and bacon...and turn them over in a few minutes...that would be great."

"Sure. No problem."

I ran upstairs and did a quick wash and dress into jeans and t-shirt. I could change into work clothes when my guests had gone. Five minutes later and we were sitting around the dining room table sharing out the food.

"So Paul, Willard, how come you're both off to Jerusalem right now?"

"Willard can tell you his story first. It's more interesting than mine."

"Well, I'm a retired doctor, and I used to work at the Saint Joseph's hospital in Denver, Colorado. One day I noticed that the front door of my next door neighbour was jammed open, and when I went to investigate I found the lady who lived there unconscious and lying on the floor. I suspected she had had a heart attack, and I managed to resuscitate her and called for an ambulance. I didn't really know Jean before that day, but I got to know her afterwards. She turned out to be an extraordinary woman. If anyone could be described as god-like, she was that woman. You know...she would talk to me about God as if he was so real to her. She was just a really impressive person. She was someone who made me remember and ponder on the Christian faith I had as a child, and into my teenage years...until life had crowded God out. Because of her witness to me I started going to church again and was hungry to discover the reality of God for myself.

"Then, about a month ago, I received a phone call from someone I knew who still worked at the hospital, saying Jean had been brought in by ambulance having had another a heart attack. I rushed into Saint Joseph's and had the honour of spending her last hours with her. For a short while she was able to talk, and she told me that she had had a vision of Jesus a few days before. In the vision he told her that she was shortly going to die, but that she would not sleep for long as Jesus was about to return. Jesus also told her that before she died, she should tell those whom he would prompt her to tell, that they should get to Jerusalem as soon as possible.

"Well, I didn't know what to make of the message about going to Jerusalem. But now I've come to understand that it's about turning the world's attention onto Jerusalem. Of course there are plenty of things going wrong in the world right now. Things that God can use to get people's attention. It's a mess. But hasn't it always been a mess? What's so different about it now? So, I didn't do anything. I hesitated. Then this star appeared in the sky, and it was as if the scales fell from my eyes. I realised that I had to at least try to get to Jerusalem. I went to the bank to buy some Israeli Shekels, then I packed my bag and went to the airport, but when I arrived I found there were no spaces for flying to Israel directly or indirectly. The woman at the airport was surprised because this is not normally a busy time of year for going to the Holy Land. So I said to the Lord, "If you want me to go to Israel then you'll have to show me the way to get there. Then the lady said to me, "There's one spare seat on a flight to Manchester airport in England, if that's any help to you?" So, I took it, and here I am."

I found his story interesting, but I wasn't entirely convinced that the events which had sent Willard off on his journey to Jerusalem were necessarily prompted by God. After all, if God really wanted Willard there why hadn't he made sure there was a spare seat available on one of the direct flights to Israel?

"So, what about you, Paul? Why are you going on this journey to Jerusalem?"

"Three things. Firstly, I have a ticket to take my car on the Eurotunnel today. I was meant to be attending an international conference in Strasbourg on supporting agriculture in Africa. Already having a train ticket is important because, like Willard, I found that all the flights from England to Israel were full up. Secondly, the conference was suddenly postponed due to a new bug that seems to be taking off, as were a number of other business meetings I had booked over the next couple of weeks. So I now had a large gap in my diary. Thirdly, I was talking to a Christian friend, who is a sort of prayer partner, about this space in my diary, and he said, "If I were you, I'd be heading off to Jerusalem right now."...and I thought, "That's exactly what I should do." Since then, God has made lots of little things happen, including prompting me to stop at Thurrock Service Station for a coffee. I met a woman I knew from years ago when I worked in Hong Kong. She was talking to Willard, and so when I heard that he too was trying to get to Israel, I said he could come with me...because when you take a car onto the train, it doesn't matter how many people are in the car."

"You're going to drive all the way to Jerusalem?"

"Well, the idea is that as we drive across Europe, we'll check on-line with any airport we go near to see if they have room on any of their flights to Jerusalem. Hopefully, we won't have to drive all the way there." Then came the punch line from Paul, "Why don't you come with us to Jerusalem? Would your company give you time off work?"

"Oh...well..." I said, searching for a reason for not going that would satisfy Paul. I'm not like Paul. I admired his willingness to 'go out on a limb', to take such a dramatic step of faith, but that wasn't me. Besides, I still hadn't decided for certain that Jesus was literally about to appear before the whole world after the church had been waiting for two thousand years. Whilst there were so many bad things happening in the world today, with the exception of the strange star appearing in the sky, the day just seemed like a perfectly ordinary day. If I told the Managing Director at work I wasn't coming in for a week or so, what reason would I give him? Whatever I told them, I knew they wouldn't understand why I was taking time off work after having given them no warning. This could end up with me losing my job, with all the financial problems that that would bring...only to find out that there was, in fact, some perfectly natural explanation for this star in the sky.

So these were my thoughts, but what I actually said to Paul was, "I don't know if it's really right for me to go. Besides, how would Jerusalem cope with having half the world descend on it, all hoping to see Jesus when he returns?" Then I paused. I didn't want to say the next thing at the front of my mind. I wasn't trying to discourage both of them...but I had to be honest with them, "Also, I expect that scientists will soon come up with a reasonable explanation for why there's a bright light circling the earth right now."

"You don't think it's a sign from God then?" Paul asked. He sounded a bit disappointed. I didn't really know how best to answer his question. Was the star a sign from God or was it some not yet understood natural phenomena. I didn't know, but my hesitation in giving an answer to his question created a break in the conversation. For a moment the only voice that could be heard was coming from my tablet in the kitchen which was set on the news channel. So it was at this exact moment that the TV news presenter said, "It has just been confirmed by the Ministry of Defence that the strange new star in the sky has stopped circling the world and has, for the last few hours, sat high up in the sky above Jerusalem." We all stopped eating and stared at one another. This was a definite 'tingles down the spine' moment. Whilst the government still had no idea what this bright light in the sky might be, they were clearly monitoring it closely, as probably every government was, and now they were telling us that it had gone to exactly the place we thought it would go to.

The three of us sat listening to the broadcast whilst we finished off our breakfast. Eventually the news program moved onto another story, and this was when I said, "Yes, Paul. To answer your question, I do believe that it is most likely a sign from God, but I won't be joining you on your journey to Jerusalem. Unlike the two of you, I have no sense that God is calling me to go there. But if you two think that he is calling you to go, then you should go."

Paul's disappointment was even more obvious now, but he didn't try to change my mind. With his car fully charged and breakfast eaten, Paul and Willard left my house and headed for Ashford to catch the Eurotunnel train to France. As soon as they had left, I rushed to get changed into my work clothes and then drove as quickly as I could to the office.

As I was driving to work, I remembered that there was a meeting taking place that morning for everyone in the company. We hadn't been told what the meeting was about, but most of my work colleagues thought that some big new deal was about to be announced which was worth a lot of money. I knew the others would be feeling pretty excited about this meeting. The Managing Director liked to keep us all happy. So in the past, whenever a really big deal was announced, he always made sure there was something in it for the rest of us. That 'something' could be anything from a bonus in our pay to an all-expenses paid day trip to Paris. He could be quite generous at times.

I was feeling pretty happy and excited during the first half of my drive to work. I reckoned I had made the right decision not to go with Paul and Willard, thereby avoiding a head-on collision with the MD. But, for the second half of the journey I wasn't feeling happy at all. I remembered a discussion that had taken place the evening before at our church gathering. One of the questions we discussed was that if Jesus really was about to return, shouldn't we be saying something to our non-Christian family, friends, neighbours, or work colleagues? Shouldn't we be warning them that the time was nearly up? Now that I was about to spend what could be our last day on earth in its present form, shouldn't I be a witness to these people, and probably in a very obvious way? My excitement turned into a sense of horror. Whilst I had never hidden the fact that I am a Christian from my work colleagues, I had previously drawn the line at doing any kind of 'in your face' evangelism. Yet time was running out and so maybe a more drastic approach was needed. Reflecting on this scenario as I finished my journey to work, I reckoned I knew exactly how it would go if I did say something to them...and as it turned out, I was right.

I arrived in my allocated parking space outside our office block just before 9:00 am. I quickly plugged in the charger, then zipped my security card to let me into the building and went to my office. Whilst my PC powered up I grabbed myself a coffee. The meeting was due to start at 9:30 am in the conference room, and sure enough there was a reminder message on my screen that the meeting was still on. I checked my phone for messages. There were now quite a few from Christian family members and friends, all of whom were coming to the same conclusion as I had, although some were more certain about this than others.

I then spent the next half an hour in a state of misery. Should I say something at the meeting with everyone being together in the same room at the same time? Surely, if they were at all interested in becoming Christians they would have asked me about it before now. I tried to do some work, but I just couldn't concentrate on anything for more than a few minutes. By the time 9:30 came my adrenaline was pumping round my body, my hands were shaking, and I was generally feeling highly stressed. Everyone else seemed to be in a very jolly mood. Certainly, the MD was all smiles as he announced the big new deal he had made with 'Provins Homes and Gardens', a French company that wanted to squeeze into the British DIY market and had a lot of money to spend on advertising. There was cake and glasses of champagne all round to celebrate. There was also much discussion about how the deal came about and who, in particular, would be working with this company. It wasn't long before the champagne was drunk, and the cake eaten, and the conversations had come to an end. So, to close the meeting the MD asked the question I was dreading, "Does anyone else have anything to say before we go back to work?"

I took in a deep breath. There was nothing for it but to do it…and so I just went for it. "Um…Yes…I want to say something, and I'm guessing that some of you, or even all of you are going to think this is a bit weird." I paused for just a moment. There was a big part of me that really did not want to say what I was about to say. A side of me that wanted nothing more than a small dark room to hide away in. But, no, this had to be done. I overrode the insistent voice that was yelling at me to run and forced myself to speak. "We all know about the star in the sky. We've all seen it on the news, and we all went outside to watch it fly over here yesterday. I know that some of you thought that it might be something to do with aliens…er…I don't really believe in aliens. But as a Christian, I do believe that one day Jesus will come back to earth…because he said he would." As I was speaking, I could see the expressions on people's faces, and I knew that this was not going down well. The one that worried me the most was Simon's face. He was one of the few people at work that I had talked directly about my faith with. He had enough religious background to understand what it meant to me. He was looking intensely at me and shaking his head, signalling, "No, don't do this," but it was too late.

"So…I just wanted to say that I, and many other Christians around the world, think the star is a sign that Jesus' return is about to happen. I just thought you should know that." The words dried up. The atmosphere was about as bad as it could be. People were either looking annoyed or amused by what I had just said. Eventually the MD said to me, "Richard, this is a business meeting, not a revival gathering. If Jesus turns up wanting us to do some marketing for him I shall be happy to discuss it with him. But I feel fairly confident that if Jesus does put in an appearance he won't be needing our help to get people's attention." It broke the ice. People started laughing, and even I thought what the MD said was quite funny. Then they began leaving the conference room to return to their own offices talking to each other as they went. So I returned to my office and found myself walking beside the guy who has the office next to mine. When he realised I was beside him he grunted and mumbled, "There's a time and a place for things," and walked on ahead of me. When I reached my office, I sat down feeling utterly deflated. But I didn't feel anxious anymore. Whether or not it had done any good, at least I had witnessed to my work colleagues and a huge burden had been lifted from me. Then, five minutes after returning to my office the MD walked in. "So, Richard, you really believe that Jesus is about to return do you?"

"Err…Yes, I think he just might."

"Just might? That doesn't sound very certain."

"History and the Bible tells us that no one can be certain about the day or the hour. There have been quite a few people who have fallen on their faces by trying to predict when it was going to happen. I'm not trying to do that. What I was trying to say was that I think the star may be a sign that he's on his way. Just as the star at Christmas over Bethlehem sort of announced the first time that Jesus came into the world. Maybe the scientists will come up with a good reason for why this is happening, but until they do, that is what I believe it is…a sign or an announcement. So, I thought that I should warn you all about this."

"Hmmm," said the MD thoughtfully. "My wife is a Christian. I expect she would agree with you about the star…I shall have to ask her. But in the meantime, I don't believe in God, and I'd appreciate it if you didn't bring God into a business meeting in the future. Okay?"

"Yes."

"Good," and with that our brief conversation was over.

"Not everyone who says to me, 'Lord, Lord,' will enter the kingdom of heaven, but only the one who does the will of my Father in heaven. On that day many will say to me, 'Lord, Lord, did we not prophesy in your name, and cast out demons in your name, and do many deeds of power in your name?' Then I will declare to them, 'I never knew you; go away from me, you evildoers.'"

Matthew 7: 21 – 23 NRSV

Chapter Five – Tuesday afternoon

For the rest of the day I stayed in my office as much as possible. During my lunch break Simon came in to talk...perhaps 'remonstrate' is a better word...but I wasn't in the mood for that kind of conversation. I was feeling far too angry with myself, but also with my fellow workers. Circumstances had conspired to make me look like a fool, and I was feeling defensive (or perhaps I should say 'offensive') about it. So, anyway, my short conversation with Simon began with him saying something like this:

"I couldn't believe you said what you did at the meeting this morning."

"Oh, hello Simon. Nice of you to drop in. What can I do for you?"

"I said, I cannot believe that you said what you said at the meeting this morning."

"I see." I waited a moment for effect. "And how can I help you to believe it?"

"What?" There was a baffled pause…then Simon continued. "You know more than most, with your Theology degree, that people have thought many times the Messiah was about to come…but he didn't."

"Yes, Simon, that is quite correct." There was another pause whilst I wondered how much of an effort I was willing to make with Simon. In the few talks Simon and I had about God, and things related, I never had the impression he was truly seeking God. It seemed to be more a matter of intellectual curiosity for him. "Well, if I'm wrong about Jesus coming…I'm wrong," I said. "As you say, I won't be the first."

With that, Simon seemed to lose interest in the conversation. He obviously felt he had made his point and seeing someone else he wanted to talk to pass my door (There are windows in our office doors), he left.

Later on that afternoon, I had a more worthwhile conversation with the newest member of staff in the company. His name was Craig, and he put his head round my door as he was leaving work.

"Hi…Richard…can we talk for a moment."

"Sure" I said. As far as I could tell he didn't look like he was angry with me. "Come in."

Craig shut the door behind him and sat down on the only spare chair in my office. "I go to church," he said rather hesitantly. I took it that he was telling me he was a Christian, but I thought I'd press him to clarify the point.

"So….you're a Christian?"

"Yes, I am. I didn't realise there was another Christian in the company."

I admitted to Craig that I wasn't very good at being a witness to the people I work with. "I tend to assume that most people will figure it out sooner or later…or if one of them knows, the word will get round. And I have always been happy to discuss the subject with anyone who wants to. However, they're not very interested, so it would seem. But now there are two of us." I smiled reassuringly at him. "Where do you go to church, Craig?"

"Christ Church in Tunbridge Wells."

"Yes, I know it. Been there only once for a wedding...I liked it." So, for a while, Craig and I talked about our Christian journeys. But it was getting late in the day, and I had work that needed doing before I went home. So I said to Craig, "Is there something I can do for you?" and Craig jumped straight in.

"It was just that I have been thinking all day about what you said in the conference room and, I guess, it's stressed me out a bit."

I smiled, "It stressed me out too!"

"Well I've been following the story on the news about the star in the sky. But it had never occurred to me that this might be a sign that Jesus is about to appear. I don't know if I am personally ready for that to happen right now."

"What do you mean when you say you are not 'ready'?"

"Well, if we suppose that Jesus were to come, bringing judgement onto at least half the world. What if he decides that I'm not good enough for him? What if I find myself in the wrong half?"

"How good do you think you need to be?"

"I don't know." said Craig, and in that moment I could tell from his expression and the sound of his voice that this was a serious issue for him.

"Measuring someone's goodness can be very difficult. If there was a chart for goodness, where would any of us place ourselves on it...assuming we were being honest? But, more importantly, where would God decide to mark the point that determines whether we are good enough or not?

"The way I see it is that Jesus died on the cross so that yours or my goodness, or lack of it, need not be the defining issue. Which means that the question Jesus asks is not, "How good are you?" If that was the question then many people, like the slave trader, John Newton, who wrote the hymn 'Amazing Grace', would never have stood a chance of being saved. I'm assuming Craig, you haven't done worse things than slave traders?"

"I don't think so."

"No. So, the question Jesus really wants the answer to is, "Do you want to be my friend?" And as he searches each of our hearts, as only God can, Jesus discovers the true answer to that question. Because when he examines our hearts he either sees someone who's really looking for God…longing for a relationship with Him, or else he finds no love or desire in their hearts for that relationship. So then, Craig, when you examine your own heart, what do you see?" I pointed at his heart. "Is there a longing in there for God?"

Craig hesitated for a moment, but then said, "Yes. I wish it were stronger, but I think it's there."

"Then that will be enough for God. The question of your being good enough is truly irrelevant. Jesus didn't say, those who are good enough will find God. He said those that seek God will find him, (Matthew 7: 7-8) and we seek because we have that longing for a relationship with him. Does that describe you, Craig?"

"Yes, I guess it does." Craig was looking quite a bit happier now.

We talked some more, and then parted with a handshake. We both felt the gravity of the moment. Either I had misread the significance of this strange star above Jerusalem, in which case we would see each other again the next day, or we were quite literally at the end of this world as we knew it.

On the off chance that this world might still be around tomorrow, I decided to finish the work I needed to do that day. For some reason, I also felt the need to sort out a few files and do a general tidy up of my office before I got into my car and drove home in silence. I didn't even have the radio on to hear the latest news. I just wanted to be alone with my thoughts.

The silence in the car didn't last very long. About half way home and my phone rang. My mum's smiling face appeared on the OLED screen. I said, "Answer" and my mum's voice could be heard, loud and clear.

"Hello darling," she said, "I only got your email an hour or so ago."

"Which email was that mum?"

"The one about the star in the sky. I think you sent it to quite a few people yesterday. But I don't check my email every day, so I've only just read it."

"Oh, yes. What did you think?"

"Well, I suppose it could be the Bethlehem star…is that what you called it?"

"Yes."

"Coming to announce the second coming…but then again, it may not be. I'm afraid I really don't know. I'm sorry." Mum was sounding like she felt she ought to know the answer to this question…but, unfortunately, she didn't. "Now, if your father had been here, I'm sure he would have given you a much more certain answer to your question."

"I wasn't expecting you, or anyone else, to give me a definitive answer as to what this star was. I was just thinking out loud, through an email, to see what people would say."

"Well, for the whole of my life, people have been saying some sign or other meant that Jesus was about to return…and he didn't. I remember my dad, your grandpa, saying Jesus would return before man set foot on the moon…but he didn't."

"Yes…well…he's got to come some time, cos he said he would. And with the state that the world is in now, I think now would be an excellent time for Jesus to come…don't you?" I felt sure mum could hear the exasperation in my voice.

"I can't cope with the stress of all this, Richard. If he comes now, then just let him come quietly. Let's not make a big thing of it."

I thought to myself, 'Fat chance of that!'

"He came quietly the last time, mum, and even then there were three kings who came to pay their respects, and a choir of angels making a noise in the hills over Bethlehem." There was no response on the phone, so I carried on. "Mum, you have nothing to worry about. When he returns, it will be to say to you, 'Well done, good and faithful servant'[iii]. Then, I expect he'll take you to the mansion he has been preparing for you, which, because of your many good works, will be a pretty impressive and substantial villa…with an out-door swimming pool and jacuzzi…which I shall pop round and make good use of if you don't mind. But, when he comes, I doubt it will be quiet. I'm expecting loud trumpets, and lots of angels flying around. The message of the Bible seems to be that, on that great day, everyone who lives, or has ever lived, will then know who Jesus is and what he has come for."

Again, mum didn't immediately respond. And when she did say something, she spoke with a quiet voice. "You don't know the people I have wounded in one way or another during my life time," she said. "My heart is a dark place."

I have to admit, I wasn't expecting that. But I was determined to counter the way she was thinking. So I said, "St Paul thought he was the 'worst of sinners'[iv]…and he may have had some good reasons for thinking that. But I believe we'll see him in heaven…don't you?"

"Yes."

"So, don't you worry about the state of your heart, mum. Jesus has got that covered," I said.

"Well," said mum. "Maybe, you're right and this star is announcing Jesus' return. But then again, maybe you're wrong, and the star is just some strange new phenomenon. Oh dear," she said, "I don't really know what to think. I'd keep it to yourself if I were you Richard. Don't do or say anything that later you'll feel embarrassed about."

'It's too late for that' I thought to myself, and shortly after that, the conversation with my mum came to an end - just as I was driving back into Maidstone.

"Then the sign of the Son of Man will appear in heaven, and then all the tribes of the earth will mourn, and they will see 'the Son of Man coming on the clouds of heaven' with power and great glory. And he will send out his angels with a loud trumpet call, and they will gather his elect from the four winds, from one end of heaven to the other."

Matthew 24: 30-32 NRSV

Chapter Six – Tuesday evening

When I arrived home, I checked my phone for messages. There was one from my cousin Paul which read, "Hi R, Willard and I are now in southern Germany, heading for Munich. Managed to book two seats on a flight from Munich airport to Tel Aviv. Flight takes off at 8:35 this evening (local time). Paul P.S. Got just under an hour of driving and just over two hours of battery left."

"So," I thought, "their faith has paid off." I was honestly glad for them, but I still felt I had made the right decision for myself. There were no other messages, except in my WhatsApp 'Chat and Pray' group. I and a few others would normally have our weekly meet up this evening. The group started a couple of years ago when Mike and I, who were already in a prayer partnership, discovered that Rachel and Mary were doing something similar. So we decided to combine partnerships; and then Lizzie joined the group. To keep the group focussed on prayer rather than just chatting, we decided to take it in turns to pray at each quarter of an hour of the meeting.

Rachel had posted a message to the group, saying, "Oh my goodness! Death is everywhere! We must meet to pray this evening!!!!" Rachel does like to use exclamation marks! Mike had responded with, "Yes, it's a sad day." I suddenly thought, "I'm missing something important here," and turned on the TV. As soon as the screen fired up I knew what had happened. The king had died.

"Weird timing, Lord." I said out loud, and quickly typed my own message, "Yes. Should definitely meet up." That would be an evening when we had a lot to chat and pray about.

We met, as usual, in Lizzie's house. Lizzie worked as a nurse at the Maidstone hospital, and she told us that the Accident and Emergency department that day had suddenly become a lot busier than normal. But these weren't injuries caused by accidents. Many people were getting angry and having fights with their family, or friends or, indeed, anyone who happened to be passing by. There was often no obvious reason for the fight breaking out. She said that it had been like the worst Saturday night you could imagine...but on a Tuesday afternoon. We prayed about this and then it was Mike's turn to talk.

Mike worked for a large recycling business as their IT Support Manager. He managed a small team (3 men 1 woman) and today they had a coffee break together in which he raised the subject of the star in the sky. He was surprised to get such an angry and confrontational reaction to the subject. Especially when he asked if anyone thought the star had some significance. He got no answer. His work colleagues just became sullen and refused to talk about it after that.

We prayed, and then it was Rachel's time to talk. Rachel was a primary school teacher, and this morning she asked her children what they thought about the star. Several of them put their hand up to say it had caused an argument in their homes that morning. Some children started crying but they couldn't explain why. Others said that people didn't know what the star was. But one little girl, whose parents were members of our church, said her daddy had told her the world was going to end soon. Although Rachel thought that what this little girl's daddy said was true, she felt very constrained over what she could say to the children. Then, at lunchtime, the headteacher sent round a memo to all the staff saying that when discussing the star with the children, it should be treated as a science subject and definitely not a religious subject. Rachel had done what the headteacher had instructed her teachers to do, but she felt bad about not being able to have a broader discussion with the children. We prayed, and then it was Mary's turn to talk.

Mary was a manager at a large supermarket on the outskirts of Maidstone. Most of her time was spent on the shop floor. It was her job to make sure everything was happening as it should, sorting out problems with staff or customers as they arose. With the economy being in a mess, times were hard for most people these days. But everyone needed to buy food and other essentials for everyday life. Like Maidstone hospital, the supermarket was experiencing a lot more problems with the behaviour of customers and staff. They had to bring in more security personnel in order to maintain a safe environment for people to shop. There was also a small amount of panic buying, which included toilet rolls. So, for a joke, Mary had bought each of us a toilet roll, which she then distributed. More prayer. Now it was me.

I told the other four about my day. My difficult decision not to go to Israel with Paul and Willard, and then the excruciatingly uncomfortable attempt at witnessing to my work colleagues. We prayed about all these things. Then, unusually, we decided to do a quick Bible study on the book of Revelation. But it was getting late and there really was too much to go through in such a short period of time. Where to begin? Was the book written to predict the distant future, or to explain what was happening at the time and in the near future? Should the images described by the writer, John, be matched up to things we can see today or are they just symbolic? None of us were experts, and we didn't make much progress there.

It was well after 10 pm when we collectively decided to go home. I had given Rachel a lift as the house she shared with another woman was on my route to Lizzie's. The other two had come in their own cars.

Lizzie lived on a modern estate, probably not more than ten years old. It lay on the outskirts of Maidstone, and as we drove away it was as quiet as you might expect at that time of night. A few moments later and we were in an older part of town, heading towards Maidstone town centre. Rachel and I were engrossed in conversation about the day's events until I turned into a small cul-de-sac. Again, the houses were new-builds, and everything was quiet here as well. A light was on in Rachel's house, but still, I waited in my car, as I always did, until Rachel was safely inside before driving away.

I live in an older part of Maidstone. To get home I had to drive close to the town centre, cross the bridge over the river Medway, and up into the western half of the town. As I drove through the town I was surprised by how many people were walking the streets at this time on a Tuesday night. I was wondering if there was some big event happening that evening in Maidstone because the town centre really was full of people. I had to slow down quickly because people were walking out into the middle of the road. Some took no notice of my car. Some seemed to be fascinated by it. Most cars being sold now are electric, so I couldn't see why some people seemed to be so curious about my car. Then I noticed that everyone seemed to be on their own. There were no groups of people. No couples. Just individuals in what I could only describe as shabby clothes. Nobody was talking to anyone else. They were just walking with their heads down, minding their own business. I felt increasingly uncomfortable, but not yet afraid of what I saw, no one was causing any trouble, but it was just weird.

I then turned into the road where I lived, Park Street, and found there were even people pacing up or down here. The terraced houses in my road were mostly over a hundred years old, and it was normally a very quiet place, day or night. I certainly hadn't expected to see anyone here this late in the evening. But there they were, crowds of people strolling along the pavement past my old house. Suddenly, one of the men who had been walking on the pavement stepped out into the road to get round a bunch of people who were blocking his way. I slammed my foot on the brake, but I couldn't quite stop before I hit him. He rolled over the front of my bonnet and then landed on the road beside my car. I immediately pressed the door lock button, and he was quickly back on his feet and shouting at me through the window. He tried the door handle, and finding it locked, he angrily slammed his hand onto the roof of my car and marched off down the middle of the road.

I stayed where I was for about a minute before driving a little further on up the road to where my house was. I then had to wait for a natural gap in the people passing by before I could get onto the drive and park my car. The encounter with that man had left me feeling anxious and threatened by these strangers on my road. But, in general, they took no notice of me and carried on walking. So I told myself to stay calm and casually plugged the charger into the car, then I went into my house and locked the door behind me. I walked into the kitchen at the back of my house and checked the back door was still locked, and then made myself a peppermint tea. I found it was a nice thing to have before going to bed. I decided not to check what was happening on the news. That may seem strange but, at that moment in time I wanted to connect with God more than wanting a news update on the TV or radio. However, I did check my messages.

There was a message from Cousin Paul. He and Willard had made it to Israel, flying in to Tel Aviv airport, and had then persuaded a taxi driver to take them to Jerusalem. With so many people trying to get to Jerusalem, they had ended up sharing a taxi with three others, which was all a bit tight, but it reduced the cost. Jerusalem, Paul wrote, was 'absolutely heaving' with people gazing up at the star and expecting Jesus to arrive at any moment. The atmosphere was 'electric,' he said. I was pleased for him and Willard, but I didn't regret my decision. If Jesus was coming then I would see him soon enough.

I have a comfortable armchair in the bedroom at the back of the house, and I usually sat there at the end of the day, with my peppermint tea, reflecting on the events of the day and praying before going to bed. On this occasion, I can remember finishing off my tea, and putting the mug down. But then I must have fallen asleep.

"Listen, I will tell you a mystery! We will not all die, but we will all be changed, in a moment, in the twinkling of an eye, at the last trumpet. For the trumpet will sound, and the dead will be raised imperishable, and we will be changed. For this perishable body must put on imperishability, and this mortal body must put on immortality. When this perishable body puts on imperishability, and this mortal body puts on immortality, then the saying that is written will be fulfilled: 'Death has been swallowed up in victory.'"

1 Corinthians 15: 51 – 54 NRSV

Chapter Seven – Early Wednesday morning

I woke to the sound of someone knocking on my front door. I was still fully dressed. I went into the empty front bedroom and looked out of the window to see who was there. In the dark, it wasn't absolutely clear, but the person looked like an elderly woman. She was standing at my front door on her own, and I noticed that there were still people walking past my house...and it was after two in the morning! I decided to open the door and see what she wanted. As I walked down the stairs I heard the woman shout through the letter box, "George. It's me, Edith. I know you're there. I can see there are lights on." This all felt really creepy, but I reassured myself that she had probably come to the wrong house. So I opened the door and there she was, a woman who was probably in her seventies, and in the same tatty clothes as all the others.

"You're not George," she said. Then she looked past me and into the sitting room, which was clearly different to what she was expecting. "I do apologies, dearie, I think I have come to the wrong house. Sorry to have disturbed your sleep." She turned around and walked past my car towards the road. Then she stopped and turned back to face me again. "What's the name of this road, dear?" she asked.

"Park Street," I replied.

"Well, that's the street I was lookin' for," she said, "and the number on your house says 63. So, is this 63 Park Street?"

"Yes," I said, "It is."

"Well that was the number I was lookin' for." The woman started walking back towards me. "I used to live here dearie, but obviously George must have sold the house to you. Do you know where he's moved to?"

"I'm sorry," I said, "but I don't think the man I bought the house from was called George. His name was more like Patrick, or something like that. I can't remember. It was seven years ago when I bought the house."

"Oh. Okay dear. Thank you for your help." The woman stood still for a moment, and I was wondering what was going to happen next. She then looked up into the sky, and then back down at me and smiled. "You're missing the fireworks," she said, and then she strolled off, quickly mingling with the other people walking past my house.

"Fireworks?" I thought, as I closed and locked the front door again. "I would have heard if there were fireworks going off." I put her comment down to the general craziness of the evening. I wasn't feeling tired now, but I thought that I really needed to get some proper sleep as I still had to go to work in the morning. However, just before I went upstairs, I noticed through the kitchen window that there were lights flashing outside in the back garden. The old lady's words came back to me. Obviously, I hadn't been aware of any flashing lights when I was talking to her at the front door. So, I unlocked the kitchen door and stepped out into the back garden to see what was going on. Then, looking up, I noticed the sky was completely clear of clouds, which meant I could see many more stars than usual.

As I gazed up, I started noticing lights, way up high, shooting across the sky. Sometimes they flew straight, and at other times they zigzagged or flew in circles. Most of these lights were very high up, but some of them flew closer to the ground. My immediate thought was 'angels'. Although they were too far away to make out what they looked like in detail, they gave off a huge amount of light. I watched these angels going about their business for several minutes before I heard the sound of a horn[v]. It sounded a long way off, and I first thought it was a car horn, but it went on and on. Then I realised it sounded more like a trumpet than a car horn. But it was just one note, which was very slowly getting louder. I remembered the angels in the book of Revelation blowing their trumpets. Their job was to get everyone's attention to what was happening...as if the time had come.

I then had the oddest of sensations. It was not unpleasant at all, but just a little hard to explain. It was as if someone as tall as me, but very light, had come up behind me and given me a hug. But in the process of doing this, they had tripped and fallen to the ground whilst holding onto me, and yet I was still standing. I instinctively looked at the ground behind me and was shocked when I saw that there really was someone lying, unmoving, on the ground...and it was me. At this point my brain was struggling to process what was happening, which was probably why I didn't immediately notice that my feet had left the ground. One moment I was standing on the lawn watching what was going on in the sky above me, and the next, I was rising up into that night sky, whilst still looking down at my un-moving body. But I didn't look at my body for long because I quickly became fascinated by the sights and sounds below me. Lights were being switched on in almost every house, and I could hear the sound of many dogs barking. Then I noticed that I wasn't the only one rising up into the sky. As far as I could see, in all directions around me, other people were doing the same.[vi] But not everyone was leaving the ground. As I looked over the town of Maidstone I could see crowds of people still endlessly walking in the streets. Some had stopped and were looking up at those of us who were still climbing into the sky. Occasionally there was a shout from one of them, but I couldn't make out what they were saying. However, the impression I had was that these people were now walking with a greater sense of urgency. Their heads were down, lost, it seemed, in their own thoughts.

I continued to climb higher and higher into the sky. Occasionally I spotted someone I knew but they were always too far away for me to shout or wave at them. But then I noticed that I, along with everyone else, were no longer just moving upwards, we were also moving in the same direction...towards the coast. It felt like a wave in the sea had picked us all up and was carrying us along. Sometimes we slowed down a little. Sometimes we sped up. The huge crowd of people just from Maidstone were intermingling with equally large crowds who had risen up from Canterbury and Folkstone and Dover, and every place in-between.

Nobody had to tell me where we were going. I just knew for certain that we were all heading towards Jerusalem. Where else would we be going? Then a massive cloud of people from London started to catch up with us, and as I looked at them I noticed something curious. Despite there being such a vast number of people coming from London, they did not create a dark cloud. Although their bodies blotted out the light from the moon, there was a glow radiating from the head of every person in the cloud[vii]. So, although the skies were becoming full of people, it was also becoming lighter by their presence. The combination of all the followers of Jesus who were alive now, joined by all those who have lived in the past, created such a staggering number of believers of every colour and ethnic group. There were also many others who had never heard of Jesus, or understood who he was, yet whose hearts resonated with God's.[viii] John, the writer of the book of Revelation said that there would be so many people that no one would be able to count them, and I could already see what he meant[ix]. I always used to feel, as a Christian, that I was outnumbered. That I was part of a minority group of people. But now I was seeing just what a vast number of people made up that minority.

Suddenly I caught a glimpse of someone I knew. At least, I think it was him...my dad...it was hard to tell. My dad had died ten years before, but he was looking very healthy in those few seconds that I saw him. I don't think he saw me. He was clearly loving the flying judging by the look on his face. But then he was gone. For a moment I felt a great sorrow that he was gone. But I took comfort in knowing he is alive, and that someday, hopefully soon, I'll see him again.

The invisible wave continued to carry us all over the English Channel, across Europe, and on towards the rising sun, and the land of Israel. I couldn't have pointed out many landmarks on the journey, although I recognised Venice. A city in a lagoon was hard to miss from high in the sky, so I knew we were heading south along the Adriatic coast. Then we crossed what I assumed was Albania and Greece, before moving out over the Mediterranean. As we flew over the sea I could see clouds of people flying in from every direction. The whole of God's people were soon to arrive at Jerusalem. Then the wave that was carrying us along turned east towards the long straight coastline of Israel. Our journey across Europe had taken very little time. At least, it felt like that. I had been taking it all in with my eyes, but I have no memory of sounds other than the sound of the wind, interspersed with the occasional shout of praise to God, or laughter. I felt sure that everyone must have been feeling the joy that I felt at that time. The joy was so wonderful, but it was nothing in comparison to what was about to come.

The mountains stood before us as we approached Jerusalem, and just like the birds as they soar on currents of warm air, so we rose up the side of those mountains. This was when I first noticed the singing...although I couldn't tell where it was coming from. It may have even been coming from inside my own head because it was a song I knew. 'Hevenu Shalom Alechem' - "We come to greet you in peace." The singing continued with this line being repeated over and over again. It was almost as if the mountains themselves were greeting us with songs. But then small groups of people around me began to sing familiar worship songs. As they did so, others joined in, sometimes singing the same song but in a different language. There was an extraordinary cacophony of songs filling the air, and as I continued my journey through the sky, so I could identify many different songs of worship and praise from around the world. The atmosphere was electric. The sky was turning into one vast stadium made up of really excited supporters waiting for their team captain to come onto the pitch. They sang their songs, they danced and waved...and then there was the most almighty roar. Of course, this wasn't a sporting event. There weren't two teams appearing before their fans. There was only one person...it was Jesus. But I'm jumping ahead a little bit here.

As we had been travelling across the skies over Europe towards Jerusalem, the trumpet that I had first heard in Maidstone had grown slowly louder, and other trumpets had joined the first. By now there were seven trumpets, each playing a different note, and together creating a wonderful harmony. As we reached Jerusalem it became clear that the trumpets were being blown from inside the star. You could hear them, but you couldn't see the angels blowing them. But then the trumpets stopped, and the last and deepest note seemed to hit me like a shockwave, which then rippled around the vast auditorium made up purely of floating, worshipping humanity.

"Then I saw a great white throne and the one who sat on it; the earth and the heaven fled from his presence, and no place was found for them. And I saw the dead, great and small, standing before the throne, and books were opened. Also another book was opened, the book of life. And the dead were judged according to their works, as recorded in the books. And the sea gave up the dead that were in it, Death and Hades gave up the dead that were in them, and all were judged according to what they had done. Then Death and Hades were thrown into the lake of fire. This is the second death, the lake of fire; and anyone whose name was not found written in the book of life was thrown into the lake of fire."

Revelation 20: 11 - 15

Chapter Eight – Jesus' arrival

Once the last note of the trumpets had been blown there was almost silence. Just the sound of a gentle breeze could be heard as we waited in anticipation for what was going to happen next. There were many angels flying up close to us now. As I watched them, they seemed to each have a purpose, though many were lining up near to the star as soldiers in a regular army would have taken up their positions, ready for the arrival of Jesus. In the pause, as we waited for the one true King, my mind started wondering where my family and friends were right now? Since the vast majority of them were Christians, I reckoned that most of them should be here, somewhere in the innumerable masses of people floating in the sky. Then I thought of my cousin Paul, and his friend Willard. Were they just on the ground in Jerusalem, or had they risen into the sky like the rest of us? I thought it would be a bit unfair if they hadn't had this experience.

Suddenly, the seven trumpet-blowing angels flew in a line out of the star, and each were still holding their trumpets. It was clearly time for

Jesus to make an appearance, and as a new trumpet fanfare began, a great roar filled the air which just kept on growing louder and louder. I'd never heard anything so loud before...and yet, strangely, it didn't hurt my ears. But it wasn't just the roar of the crowd that impacted on me, it was also the joyful, and even ecstatic expressions on people's faces as they danced and waved and clapped. I didn't have to explain to myself why these people were doing what they were doing, because I was doing exactly the same. It was as if this was the only appropriate way to behave under the circumstances, and I was particularly conscious that I had the most enormous grin on my face.

That was the moment when something changed in me. I found myself experiencing a roller-coaster of emotions. For a moment, I lost my joy and I started to weep like I've never wept before. At first my weeping was for myself. For the mistakes I had made. For the times when I could have done good, but I did bad instead. Times when I hurt someone rather than helped them. For the cruel and harsh words I could never take back. For the toxic soup of lust and greed and selfishness and laziness and secret desires for corrupted things. It all came pouring out of me through my tears. But my attention could not be on me for long when I was surrounded by so many people. Still, my tears continued to flow. How many centuries of suffering, injustice and heart ache had humanity endured? Every kind of wickedness. Every form of torture. Every horror that people had found themselves capable of inflicting on their fellow human beings. Every sickness. Every act of greed. Every nightmare that made life a misery for so many people. Were those days really over? The days of darkness, gone? YES THEY WERE! The days of light were breaking forth, just as the sun rose over the mountains of Judea. And so my tears ceased, and laughter took over as I was hit by a wave upon wave of love and joy, and love and joy, and love and joy, and so on. I had never experienced such an explosion of emotions. This was a good day indeed! No wonder I was grinning like a clown, and I couldn't stop myself from laughing more than I had ever done before.

It's funny how my brain worked during all of this. There were moments when I was simply lost in the sights and sounds of everything going on around me...and really not thinking at all. Then I'd get a flash of inspiration. Like when it suddenly occurred to me that, in our singing, dancing and cheering, we were doing exactly the same as the disciples did when Jesus rode into Jerusalem on a donkey two thousand years before. The main difference being that there were billions more people this time. History was repeating itself, only on a much larger scale. So large, in fact, that my description of it can only be inadequate. It's hard to describe an experience as extreme as this when I have had no similar experience that I could possibly compare it with...and then Jesus came out of the star. Not on a donkey....but on a throne...and I remembered Jesus' own words to the Sanhedrin before he was nailed on the cross, "You will see the Son of Man sitting at the right hand of the Mighty One and coming on the clouds of heaven."[x] I doubt I was the only person who remembered those words in that moment, as Jesus and his throne came out of that star, both full of light.

As he descended towards Jerusalem[xi], surrounded by a troop of angels who were staying close by him, I could hear a new sound. Whilst those of us who were flying much higher than Jesus now was experienced nothing more than a gentle breeze, looking down at Jesus and his angels, you could see that the air had started to swirl around them. Then, as they drew nearer to the earth, the encircling wind was turning into a major cyclone. At this point the angels left Jesus and rose to be up above the cyclone. But Jesus, being at the centre of the swirling wind, was unaffected by it. So, as we watched, Jesus continued his descent to the ground. Now, I thought, we shall see something more of the power of God, and so we did. The closer Jesus got to the ground, the more powerful the cyclone became. The swirling cloud around Jesus then became lit up with flashes of lightening, and out of the cloud came peels of thunder. Then, as Jesus was about to land on the ground, the vast cloud of witnesses, of which I was just a tiny part, could no longer keep themselves from joining in. The roar that came from our mouths just grew and grew, louder and louder. Now, with the combined sound of the angels with their trumpets, the thunder coming from the circling clouds around Jesus, and the myriad of people who had put their trust in Him, was both joyful, and utterly deafening. It was sheer brilliance!

When Jesus landed in the centre of Jerusalem with the cyclone still spinning around him, two amazing things happened. Firstly, when the throne landed gently on the earth behind Jesus, it triggered a great earthquake in the ground around the throne. But it was a strange sort of earthquake because out from the ground, all around Jesus and his throne, the cyclone and earthquake merged to create a huge wave of fire and water which grew upwards from the ground around Jesus. For a moment I lost sight of him as the wave rose up like a tower, higher and higher above the ground. This was the wave of life and death that, with a very loud 'bang', it suddenly exploded and shot out all directions away from Jesus. Every person or other part of the created order that was destined to remain, was left untouched or even restored by this rolling tidal wave. Everyone and everything destined to be destroyed, vanished into the sea of fire and water that we could see rushing away in all directions. Land that was polluted was restored to its unpolluted state. The seas were made clean, as were the rivers and lakes. In almost no time at all, after the wave of fire and water had left Jerusalem to do its work around the whole world, so the land behind the wave settled. The cyclone dissipated and there was peace. The calm after the storm. From that day onwards there would never be another earthquake again.

The second amazing thing that happened, just as the wave of fire and water shot out from around Jesus and his throne, whilst still reaching up high into the sky, so the star above Jerusalem began to descend slowly. As it did so, the single white light began to fizz and sparkle into many lights and a myriad of colours. It wasn't at first clear what was happening, but then the people understood, and there was a collective 'Oooh' sound, like when people watch fireworks, as the star was transformed into the new city of Jerusalem. This was the heavenly city which would unite with what remained of the earthly city of Jerusalem.

The two became one. Now it was the home city for Jesus and the spiritual capital for the world…and the beauty of the new Jerusalem was incredible.

With the wave of fire and water now disappeared over the horizon, and the two cities united, the next thing I saw was a stream of crystal clear water pouring out from under Jesus' throne. The volume of water didn't seem that great near the throne, but as the stream ran away from the throne, so the water got deeper. Before long the water had become a wide river which flowed gently down the middle of a grand new main street of Jerusalem[xii]. All these things happened with the trumpets still sounding out their fanfares, but they were more subdued now. The main event was over. But, still, the vast crowds of people kept on breaking into spontaneous applause and there were still lots of loud cheers which rippled around the huge auditorium, still full of flying people.

No doubt there are many details I have missed out in this story. With so many people around it was hard to see everything. But whilst the sense of excitement was still there, it was definitely passed its peak. Whilst many angels continued to rush here and there with some task or other to perform, there was nothing for me to do. For a while I continued to enjoy my experience of flying. But it wasn't long before I realised I was losing height, and eventually I landed on my feet in the middle of Jerusalem. The atmosphere around me was still electric…incredibly alive and joyful. Understandably, everyone wanted to get close to Jesus, but the angels were keeping things under control. I saw glimpses of him as he met so many people, but I knew that my turn to meet him would come some day and I was content to wait for that day. In the meantime, I decided that I would take a stroll around the city and gaze at its beauty and maybe meet someone I knew. This was a great day indeed!

"And I heard a loud voice from the throne saying,

'See, the home of God is among mortals.
He will dwell with them;
they will be his peoples,
and God himself will be with them;
he will wipe every tear from their eyes.
Death will be no more;
mourning and crying and pain will be no more,
for the first things have passed away.'"

Revelation 21: 3-4 NRSV

Chapter Nine – New beginning

It was several hours later when I found my cousin Paul. I had been wandering around the new Jerusalem, and I saw him just as I reached the river flowing out from under the throne of God. He was wading out into the river. He had managed to find a snorkel from somewhere and was about to try it out. He wasn't the only person swimming in the river. There were lots of others enjoying the cool, clear water. I called out to him and he smiled and waved, then started wading towards me.

"So you made it to Jerusalem," he said.

"I came by air," I replied. "Have you lost Willard?"

"Yes, in that size crowd it was easy to lose people. But the good news is that in this new world nobody ever gets lost. I could find him if I needed to."

"I saw my dad," I said, "when we were flying to Jerusalem…I only caught a glimpse of him, but he looked like he was having a great time. I'm sure I'll bump into him sooner or later. Have you seen your dad?"

"No, I haven't yet."

"There was a huge crowd of people who went off to the beach at Tel Aviv. Your dad always liked the beach so he may have gone there. You should check it out."

"I will, but first I want to check out the fish in this river."

I sat down beside the river and watched Paul swimming around amongst the fish. They didn't seem bothered by him at all. Even when Paul touched the fish they just ignored him. Fortunately, the water was so clear I could easily see the beautiful multi-coloured fish without needing to stick my head under the water.

Amongst the changes that were already tangible was the change in attitude people had about time, which was much more relaxed in comparison to that of our old life. There seemed to be a general acknowledgement that we now live in a world where there was no reason for hurrying to do anything. So, for some time Paul and I hung out together. We spent our days either swimming in the river or talking to the people who strolled along beside the river. There was a new sense of freedom in our talking to complete strangers. It seemed like everyone had a story to tell and they had lost the need to be wary about what they said to others. They would open up to us about the story of their lives before Jesus returned. They had come for healing and, as we sat with them in the warm sun, our feet dangling in the flowing water, we would pick and eat the fruit of the miraculous trees that had sprung up so quickly along the river bank. It was such a joy and privilege to be there, and to watch these people walk away with a brighter smile and a greater sense of peace about them.

In the evening, it quickly grew dark, and although it was cooler at night than in the day, it was never particularly cold. On our first night in the new Jerusalem, someone told us to go to a place that has since become known as Pilgrim Square. When we got there we found an angel was standing in the middle of the square. He was holding a large sack, and with a big smile on his face, he handed out sleep mats and blankets to anyone who needed them.

When Paul and I had both been given our mat and blanket, we studied them closely. The mat seemed to offer very little cushion for sleeping on the ground, and the blanket was very thin. Paul and I talked about pretending we hadn't already got a sleep mat and blanket so we could ask the angel for another one each. I was very glad we didn't. We found out later that if you take a hard sleeping mat and add some 'miraculous' to it, it turned out to be very comfortable throughout the night. Or take the thinnest of blankets and add some 'miraculous' to it and it will keep you warm in the coldest of weather. But, together, they were very light and could be easily rolled up and carried with you. They didn't wear out, and nobody ever stole them from us. It took us a while, along with many experiences in which we found this to be true, to really appreciate the fact that we now lived in the world of the miraculous.

There was also a great spirit of generosity with everyone we met, and there were many nights when people invited us into their homes to eat with them. They often had a spare room for us to sleep in as well. Paul and I would insist that they didn't need to make up a bed for us because we had our mats and blankets. But people wanted to be generous to others as they had experienced the generosity of their heavenly Father to them.

Then one day, Paul and I bumped into Willard. By chance, he had met up with a group of people who were also from Denver, Colorado, and he was having a wonderful time. However, he was beginning to wonder if he should be going home. "I think we're in a honeymoon period right now," he said, "but there will soon be work for everyone to do." I hadn't thought much about that before. I always equated the new heaven and new earth as a place of non-stop fun. "So, would they be needing doctors now in this new world?" I asked. Willard didn't know. But he felt certain that his heavenly Father was wanting him to return home, so that is what he was going to do. Paul and I both hugged Willard and prayed for the Father's blessing on the life he now had ahead of him.

Thinking back to that time, it's strange that I asked so few questions about how life now worked in this new environment. For example, I didn't for a moment wonder how Willard was going to get back to Denver, which was, I presumed, still on the other side of a huge ocean. I just took it as a given that if Willard said he was going to Denver...then that was where he was going. We were all now living in a period of transition, and it was only gradually that I came to realise how life was different in the new world. It wasn't just the addition of the 'miraculous' that I mentioned before. There was a whole mindset that needed to change. I must admit that I found it quite difficult to move from the old-world mindset that everything is temporary, to the new-world mindset in which life is now forever. There were lots of assumptions that I had to re-think about this new world. I had assumed everyone entered heaven healed of every wound, physical or emotional. Yet the trees alongside the river bore fruit which were for healing, and the promise of scripture was not that we would have no tears, but that God would wipe away the tears we had(Revelation 21).

I felt like a child all over again, wanting answers to all my questions. As a child, my dad was the one who used to answer those questions. It was the role he had played when I was growing up and I was missing his wisdom now. I talked with God about it, and my prayer was heard. About two weeks after parting with Willard, I was heading for the beach in Tel Aviv where I was due to meet up with Paul and a group of friends for some fun and relaxation. The streets were quiet and so it was easy to pick up the sound of a debate going on in the garden of a house I was passing. The discussion seemed to be about the book of Joel in the Bible. There was an archway in the garden wall, and when I reached it I stopped to look into the garden. There were about twenty men and women sitting in the shade of several trees and taking it in turns to speak. An elderly looking man saw me and beckoned me to come in and sit on a chair beside him and listen to the debate. I must have been sat on that chair for two or three minutes before the person who was sitting on the other side of me quietly said, "Excuse me, but do I know you?" I turned to look at him, and then said in a far too loud a voice, "Dad!"

I always say that it was the lack of glasses which made me miss the fact that I had just sat down next to my dad without realising that he was there. He had always worn thick glasses, and now he didn't need to. He had perfect vision. We left the garden at his suggestion and then had a big hug outside. We both wanted to talk and so we found a bench down near the beach to sit on. He looked older than I had expected to see him. "I always thought everyone in heaven would be about the optimum human age of somewhere between 25 – 30 years old, but you look a lot older than that."

My dad laughed. "Thank you Richard... but you look older than 30 years too. I think the way it works is that you never stop growing older in heaven, but neither do you ever lose your strength or energy. So then, one day you'll be an 80 year old in a 25 year old's body, and so on."

I laughed at the thought. "So what will we look like when we're a million years old?"

"I don't know," Dad said. "More like God, hopefully."

There was a brief lull in the conversation as we watched people on the beach. Then I said quietly, "I didn't die, Dad. I never had that experience. I was one of those who was still alive when Jesus returned. Something strange happened to me in my back garden, just before I flew up into the sky. I didn't really think about it then because there was just so much going on. But later, I decided that it must have been the moment when my old body dropped off me and it was my new body which rose up into the air. So, it's strange to say this but I wonder if I had somehow missed out on the experience of death."

"Dying felt just like falling asleep," my dad said. "The build up to it could be unpleasant, but the experience of dying itself was just one of losing consciousness...like you do when you fall asleep every night. I woke up like everyone else on the day Jesus came back to earth. I found myself rising up into the sky, like you, with a new body. So you didn't actually miss much by not dying."

"Did you dream at all when you were asleep?"

"I think I did once. It was hard to tell, and I can barely remember it now. It may have only been a memory from my previous life. Your Uncle Reg told me he had quite a few dreams so he might be a better person to ask about that."

"You've seen Uncle Reg? I don't think Paul has seen him yet. Paul is down on the beach," I pointed. "He's with that group playing volleyball. The one with the white hat."

"I can see him...and I think I know where Reg is. I'll go and get him. He'll be very pleased to see Paul."

"But first, Dad, there's one more question I want to ask you." I then found myself instinctively looking around to check no one was listening. It felt like I was doing something wrong in asking the question, but I was sure this was a question that was sitting at the back of everyone's minds.

 "What has happened to all those who rejected God?" I asked in almost a whisper.

"They're gone."

"What do you mean "they're gone"?"

"They've just gone. They are no more."

"So they're not sitting somewhere in an eternal torment?"

"No. As I understand it, they're not. Such a place does not exist. There is only the new heaven and the new earth, which have come together to form one home for everyone. There is now only light in this new world. There is no darkness. Satan and his angels are all gone. Defeated and destroyed. The corrupted earth has been renewed and made incorruptible...like you and me, and there is now no limit to the relationship we can have with God."

The conversation with my dad left me feeling relieved and content, just as those I had with him when I was a child had done. We talked a little longer, and then he went to find Uncle Reg. Meanwhile, I joined

Paul and the others on the beach. It had been quite a while since I had played beach volleyball, but everyone's attitude was that the fun of playing was far more important than the winning. Ten minutes later I had the joy of watching Uncle Reg give Paul lots of hugs and kisses. I had never seen the two of them be so demonstrative. Paul left the game and walked off down the beach with his dad, talking and laughing and generally enjoying each other's company. The rest of us carried on playing. There was no rush to finish the game. We all had people we wanted to see, to spend time and catch up with. We all had things we wanted to do…God-given dreams we wanted to pursue. But we also knew that we now had eternity ahead of us to discover the inner depths of God, to experience life in all its fulness, and to explore the whole of God's creation that we call the Universe.

THE END

Addendum

This story is a work of fiction. I cannot possibly know how the world as it currently exists will end. Nor can I predict when it will happen. So is there much point in my writing a story which attempts to predict the future? Our ability to imagine is an important aspect to our spiritual journey. Those in authority in Israel at the time of Jesus lacked the imagination to see something of God in the man standing before them. When they looked at Jesus, all they could see was a man who was causing them trouble and who needed to be got rid of. When Jesus was arrested and put on trial before the Sanhedrin, at the pinnacle moment of this crisis he tried to awaken their imagination. In his Gospel, Mark describes the moment when the High Priest asks Jesus if he is the Messiah[xiii]. Jesus answers, "I am; and 'you will see the Son of Man seated at the right hand of the Power,' and 'coming with the clouds of heaven.'" But his effort to awaken their imagination is in vain and the Sanhedrin condemned Jesus to death. So, this story is an exercise in me using my own imagination in the hope that others will be enabled to think more deeply about what the second coming of Jesus would mean to them. It's quite Ignatian actually!

Probably the biggest use of the imagination in this story is the picture of billions of people flying through the skies to Jerusalem to meet and witness the return of the king...King Jesus. This rising up into the sky is called the Rapture. Many Christians believe that the Rapture is the way that God will rescue the believers from a world that is about to get very bad indeed (known as the Tribulation), but I'm not one of them. So, here is why I don't believe in this divine rescue. 1) We don't have to look to the future to imagine how the Tribulation will be. If we have some idea about the carnage of the 20th century, for example, with its two World Wars, and numerous other revolutions, wars, famines, disasters, persecutions and atrocities in every corner of the world, there should be enough evidence to argue that we are already in the time of Tribulation. 2) The key Bible passage is 1 Thessalonians 4: 16-

17, "For the Lord himself, with a cry of command, with the archangel's call and with the sound of God's trumpet, will descend from heaven, and the dead in Christ will rise first. Then we who are alive, who are left, will be caught up in the clouds together with them to meet the Lord in the air; and so we shall be with the Lord forever." The important words in this passage are 'to meet the Lord in the air'. We are not rising up to fly from the world's problems. We are rising up to welcome Jesus as he is descending, just as there were probably many people who came out of Jerusalem to welcome Jesus riding into the city on a donkey. 3) In the 20 centuries since Jesus walked this earth, do we see a pattern of God intervening to enable believers to escape the horrible events of human history? I'm sure that, on occasions, this did happen to individuals or small groups of people (Peter was an example of this happening[xiv]), but it is not the norm (Peter was later executed so this act of saving him was only temporary). What is far more common is the calling of God for his people to suffer alongside others who are suffering. To be courageous in standing up for the poor and needy, in speaking out against those who persecute and destroy the lives of others. This can be a very dangerous thing to do, but our calling is to take the suffering which may come our way, in order to establish more of God's kingdom on this earth. There is no escaping the Tribulation!

Some people, reading this story, might be troubled by the apparent lack of a Judgement day, and of hell. Well, I don't see that a Judgement day has to take up much time. In the human justice system there needs to be a period of time for evidence to be collected and processed before there is a trial. The assumption is that the person is innocent until proven guilty, and it may take a lot of time to prove their guilt. But it is not like that with God. He already knows everything about us. He knows if we are guilty or innocent, and whether or not we live under the protection that comes through Jesus' death on the cross. So, in my story, judgement takes place as the wave of water and fire shoots out from Jerusalem and goes around the world simply destroying those people and things which have been destined for destruction. There is no need for the story to consume any more time than that.

The subject of hell is a little more controversial because it is an idea which is so thoroughly ingrained in our thinking...yet I believe that it is a false idea. So, let me start by saying that I am a Conditionalist when it comes to the doctrine of hell. Whereas a Traditionalist would argue that all people were created and born to live for eternity, so that the only question is where will we spend that eternity (in heaven, hell, purgatory?), the Conditionalist would say we were not created eternal, but that at some point in our lives we are born of the Spirit and this is what enables us to live for eternity in God's Kingdom. Eternal life is therefore conditional on us entering into a relationship with God, in which case God will then 'know' us and welcomes us into his Kingdom. So, for a Conditionalist, there is no need for an alternative place for people to go as they have never been given the gift of eternal life. Here are some helpful Bible passages which, in my view, support this idea[xv].

But there are other reasons why I don't believe in hell, and these are a few of them. 1) The idea of hell doesn't make any sense to me. This is because whatever someone may have done wrong, or however wicked they are, there is an injustice in putting them into a place where they will experience conscious suffering for eternity. At some point in their suffering they must have been punished enough and then they should be removed from hell, but they aren't. The church argued this point by saying that all sin is against God. Then they took the ancient Roman legal system which held that the seriousness of a crime was in part-way determined by who the crime was committed against. So to steal an apple from a poor man was not too serious, but stealing an apple from a Roman Senator was very serious. In this way, to commit an offence against God himself is so bad that it somehow justifies eternal conscious suffering. But I would argue that the Roman legal system was not, first and foremost about justice. It was more to do with maintaining the place at the top of society for the rich and powerful. Therefore, I don't consider this to be a valid argument. 2) The imagery of hell is often that of fire, like the fire of Gehenna, or the lake of fire in Revelation 20: 11-15. This is a curious choice of imagery for the traditional idea of hell, because although the person who is burnt by the fire experiences great suffering, it can never be eternal conscious suffering. The burning is brought about by the consuming nature of fire. It destroys as it burns. A person being burnt by the fire will quite quickly die in the fire. There is nothing eternal about being burned. The fire might be eternal and never go out, but the thing it is burning will not be. A better illustration for the traditional idea of hell would be a torture chamber where the idea is to make life very painful for the person without actually killing them. But this is not used to illustrate hell in the Bible. 3) The idea of hell makes me suspicious that it is a human construct. Faced by the calling of God to draw all people into the kingdom, I could imagine the discussion amongst Christian leaders as they decided to take a 'carrot and stick' approach to evangelism. The 'carrot' is heaven, with all its associated good things, and the 'stick' has to be the worst possible thing that can happen to anyone...eternal conscious suffering. So, whilst I cannot guarantee that there is no hell, I find the idea of a second death (from which there is no coming back) to be far more likely[xvi].

---

[i] Genesis 1: 31 God saw everything that he had made, and indeed, it was very good. And there was evening and there was morning, the sixth day.

[ii] Isaiah 11: 06 The wolf shall live with the lamb, the leopard shall lie down with the kid, the calf and the lion and the fatling together, and a little child shall lead them.

[iii] Matthew 25: 21 His master said to him, "Well done, good and trustworthy slave; you have been trustworthy in a few things, I will put you in charge of many things; enter into the joy of your master."

[iv] 1 Timothy 1: 15 The saying is sure and worthy of full acceptance, that Christ Jesus came into the world to save sinners—of whom I am the foremost.

^v 1 Thessalonians 4:16   For the Lord himself will come down from heaven, with a loud command, with the voice of the archangel and with the trumpet call of God, and the dead in Christ will rise first.

^{vi} 1 Thessalonians 4: 17   After that, we who are still alive and are left will be caught up together with them in the clouds to meet the Lord in the air. And so we will be with the Lord forever.

^{vii} 2 Timothy 4:8   Now there is in store for me the crown of righteousness, which the Lord, the righteous Judge, will award to me on that day—and not only to me, but also to all who have longed for his appearing.

^{viii} Romans 2: 13 – 16 For it is not the hearers of the law who are righteous in God's sight, but the doers of the law who will be justified. When Gentiles, who do not possess the law, do instinctively what the law requires, these, though not having the law, are a law to themselves. They show that what the law requires is written on their hearts, to which their own conscience also bears witness; and their conflicting thoughts will accuse or perhaps excuse them 16on the day when, according to my gospel, God, through Jesus Christ, will judge the secret thoughts of all.

^{ix} Revelation 7:9   After this I looked, and there before me was a great multitude that no one could count, from every nation, tribe, people and language, standing before the throne and before the Lamb. They were wearing white robes and were holding palm branches in their hands.

^x Matthew 26: 64 Jesus said to him, "You have said so. But I tell you. From now on you will see the Son of Man seated at the right hand of Power and coming on the clouds of heaven."

^{xi} Acts 1: 10 – 11   They were looking intently up into the sky as he was going, when suddenly two men dressed in white stood beside them. "Men of Galilee," they said, "why do you stand here looking into the sky? This same Jesus, who has been taken from you into heaven, will come back in the same way you have seen him go into heaven."

^{xii} Revelation 22:1 – 2   Then the angel showed me the river of the water of life, as clear as crystal, flowing from the throne of God and of the Lamb down the middle of the great street of the city. On each side of the river stood the tree of life, bearing twelve crops of fruit,

yielding its fruit every month. And the leaves of the tree are for the healing of the nations.

xiii Mark 14: 61-62

xiv Acts 12: 6-19

xv Genesis 3: 22-24, Matthew 7: 21 – 23, John 3: 1-21.

xvi Revelation 20: 14 - 15

Printed in Great Britain
by Amazon

42537219R00050